CW00370099

Dear Mum

Dear Mum

Katy Simmons

CONSTABLE

Constable & Robinson
55-56 Russell Square
London WC1B 4HP

This edition published by Constable,
an imprint of Constable & Robinson Ltd 2012

Copyright © Katy Simmons 2012
Illustrations © Leah Barker 2012

All rights reserved. This book is sold subject to the condition
that it shall not, by way of trade or otherwise, be lent, re-sold,
hired out or otherwise circulated in any form of binding or
cover other than that in which it is published and without a
similar condition including this condition being imposed on
the subsequent purchaser.

A copy of the British Library Cataloguing in Publication Data
is available from the British Library

ISBN-13: 978-1-47210-649-0

Designed and typeset by Design 23, London
Printed and bound by CPI Group (UK) Ltd, Croydon, CR0 4YY

1 3 5 7 9 10 8 6 4 2

Introduction

When I packed all three of my daughters off to their grandmother's house for a few days during their summer holidays in order to get some work done in peace and quiet, I expected to talk to them on the phone, I knew that my eldest would send me a text now and again, I was even thinking about getting Granny to set up Skype – but I never expected them each to send me a lovely letter…

I realised right away that Granny must be responsible. Letters are such old-fashioned things, after all … or are they? When I told my friends about the letters, I soon realised that writing to Mum isn't such a rare occurrence for other kids who are away from home. Some are encouraged to write letters from school while others like to leave notes around the house for their mothers to find. And plenty of those mothers tend to keep their precious letters somewhere safe to read again later on (or perhaps to embarrass their children with when they are grown up!)

Of course, when embarking on the huge task of writing a letter, you don't waste too much time on trivia. Letters are for important stuff – and it's what the children who wrote the letters that are featured in this book found important that make them so fascinating to read. Some of them are simple messages of love. Some are despatches from a child who is missing their mother. Some are promises, apologies, or requests for presents or favourite meals. And some are just funny little thoughts that needed to be put down on paper.

We have printed these letters pretty much exactly as the children wrote them. However, while some of the grammar is still erratic, we did decide to tidy up the spelling rather than leaving some of the original versions in – charming as some of those were, we felt it was better for the reader not to be distracted by spelling mistakes.

The thing I have really enjoyed about compiling these letters is the way that each one tells its own little story and gives us a tiny window into the way a child sees the world.

Dear Mum,

Thanks for being such a brilliant mum and for doing lots of fun things with us.

When I grow up I want to be as nice as you!

From

Tim

Dear Mum

Happy Mother's Day.

You deserve a special day. You always do nice things for me when I am sad and when we play together you make me happy. Sorry I didn't tidy my room. I will do it all the time now so you don't have to.

Have a happy happy day.

From Ellie

Dear Mum,

Here is a picture of Tiger. He is looking sad because you are not here to put him to bed, but he knows you are looking after Grandma so he is happy about that.

We are doing fine. We have been on time to school every day. Dad's cooking is fine but you make nicer spaghetti than him.

I hope Grandma's leg is better soon and you can come home. I hope you are having a lovely time.

Lots of Love and Kisses,

Layla

xxxxxxxx

Sir Tiger The 1st

Dear Mum,

DON'T GO IN MY ROOM. I am making something special for you and don't want you to see it before it is finished.

(It's not because it hasn't been tidied I promise.)

I will give you the present later after school.

Love from Kim

Dear Mum,

Thank you for being my mum and giving me your nice biscuits and letting me eat the chocolate on a Saturday. I would really like it if you would let me have chocolate yesterday but Sara's mum doesn't let her have any at all so I think you're better than her mum.

Lots of Love
Tanya xxx

Dear Mum,

Thank you for encouraging me to take that part in the school play. I was very scared at first but now I really love it.

Love Susannah

xxxxxxxx

Dear Mum,

You told me that I could be anything I wanted when I grow up. I have decided that I want to be a cat.

Lots of love
Jackie
xxxxxx

Dear Mum,

I hope you have a great time at the dance.

I think you look like a princess in your new dress so I drew a picture of a princess.

We are going to make chocolate cakes while you are out so you can have some when you get back if you want.

Love and kisses,
Lottie

Dear Mum,

I think that you are very clever because you can use the iron that you say I'm not to touch because it is really hot and heavy. I hope I grow up to be like you.

Loads of Love
Angela xxxx

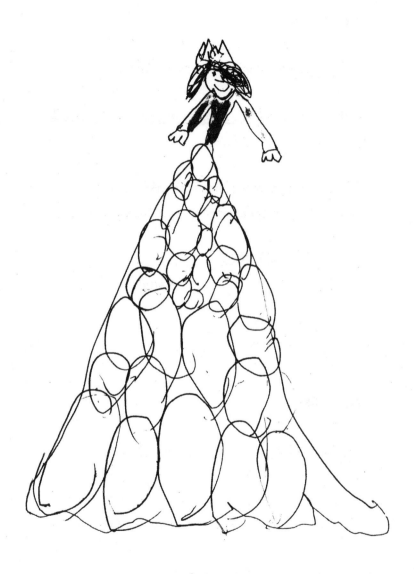

Dear Mum,

I have been playing in the snow with Aunt Carol, but I wear my new coat and boots and we have cocoa when I come in.

Grandad says hello and not to worry about the weather.

I am having fun here, but I am looking forward to coming home soon.

See you on Saturday.

Love James

PS Grandad is sending you some seeds so don't throw the envelope away. They are only little, they are from his garden and he says they will grow into big flowers if you plant them now.

Dear Mum,

Thank you so much for my birthday party last week and the bouncy castle in the garden that Tom fell off. All my friends had a really good time even though Darren threw the jelly at Pete. I did help you clean up though. Sorry about the bowl of crisps that fell onto the floor but I don't think that was our fault, it just fell off the table. I don't know why.

Love Jack   xxx

Dear Mum,

Thank you for being my mum and looking after me very well. I am happy when I come home from school and you have bought me some new biscuits. Please can Steven come to tea next Wednesday after school?

Love Jerome
xxxxxx

16

Dear Mum,

I want to tell you that I love you and I like your chocolate cake. I like it when you play with me and I'm sure that if we were the same age we would be best friends.

Love you from
Lily xxxxx

Dear Mum,

I think you are a very kind and caring person and so do my friends. You look after me very well and I like the smell of the washing powder you use to keep my school uniform clean and nice. My friends smell it at school and they like it too. I also like your red lipstick the best and when I'm grown up I'm going to have the same perfume as you. The one that you say is too expensive to use until I'm a grown up.

Lots of Love
Gina xxxxx

Dear Mum,

Thank you for being my mum. I like that you tidy my bedroom. Could I please have £5 to buy two plastic dinosaurs to fit in the jungle I am making in my bedroom?
Love Liam

Dear Mum,

You cook very nice spaghetti and my friends think so too.

Love from your little girl Tallulah
xxxxxxxx

Dear Mum,

I am sorry that I borrowed your silky scarf. I didn't mean for the cat to rip it up. We were just playing in the garden and Stella started chasing it. I will save my pocket money and get you a new one. I didn't mean to get it dirty either, that was because I tripped over the flower pot when I was chasing the cat.

Love Millie

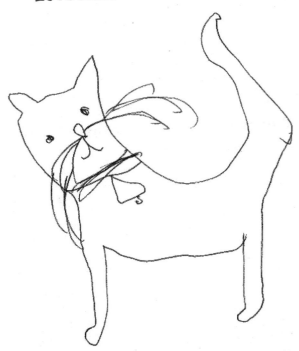

Dear Mum,

I want to tell you that I will always love you and I will never move out of our house and live away from you or drink any of your wine even when I'm a teenager. I like that you wash all my clothes and cook me nice food to eat.

I want to live with you always because you look after me so well. You are nice to me when I am sad and if I cry.

I love you almost as much as I love Smokey the cat and I really, really love him.

Love Katie

xxxxx

Dear Mum,

I am worried that you will not love me as much when you have the new baby. You might not want to spend as much time playing with me.

Grandma says that I have to be grown up because the new baby will need more looking after than I do but I feel as if I still need lots of looking after. I hope that you don't just make cakes for the new baby and not make any for me.

Please still be my mum as well.

Lots of love   Lizzie xxx

Dear Mum,

I didn't like it when you went away last weekend and left me with Grandma. I like being with Grandma but I like it better with you. Please don't go away without me again. I would like to come with you.

Love Sophie xxxxxxx

21

A dalek

Dear Mum,

Please can you buy me a Dalek for my birthday? I want a big, real one like on Dr Who. I won't let it be mean and nasty like the ones on TV I will tame it and it will be my friend and protect me from all bad people by **EXTERMINATING** them.

   Lots and lots of love
   Charlie xxxxxx

Dear Mum,

I am very sorry for being naughty and not tidying my room. I am sorry that you fell over Barbie's car and I know I should have put it away like Daddy said I should. Please don't be angry at me. I love you very much and I feel all lonely when you shout at me.

   Lots of Love
   Carrie xxxxxxxxx

Dear Mum,

Why do you always drink cups of tea before you do things? I always have to wait until you've had a cup of tea before we can do things like go to the park to play. I wish tea didn't exist.

Love from Milo

Dear Mum,

Thank you for being my mum and letting me have a puppy. I promise that I will walk him every day and make sure that he doesn't make too much mess. Please let him sleep on my bed.

Lots of love from Bradley
xxxxxxxxx

Dear Mum,

Can I please, please, please get a kitten? I will look after it everyday and it can sleep in my bed with me and it will love me very, very much because I will love it very, very much.

I will love you for ever if you let me have a kitten.

Lots of love
Ruth

Dear Mum,

I accidentally dropped your best perfume. I have hidden it in the bathroom cupboard in case you found out.

Love from
Anna
xxxxx

25

Dear Mum,

Please, please can I have a red bike for my birthday? I have always wanted one. Please can I have the one with the basket on the front so that I can put snacks in it for when I'm playing at explorers?

Love you lots and lots
Ella
xxxxxxx

Dear Mum,

Me and Gina have decided that we are
going to help you to do things round the
house. We are big enough now to do all the
washing up and I want to learn to use
the vacuum cleaner lie you do.

We are going to do this for you because
you are so kind to us.

      Lots and lots of love
      Your little girls Lisa and Gina
      xxxxxxxxx

Dear Mum,

I have lost my best gloves somewhere on the way
to school or coming home from school. I might have
left them at school but I can't remember. Please don't
be angry with me. I hope I still get some Christmas
presents. I have tried to find them but I can't.

I am very sorry
     Love from Sally xxxxxxx

Dear Mummy

I want you to know that I think you're the best mummy ever. I always think that. Please teach me how to wash dishes and use the washing machine because that looks like fun.

Love you Georgia

Dear Mum,

I am sorry that I forgot my football kit at school. Please don't be angry. I don't mind wearing it next week even if it is all dirty.

Love from
Johnny xxx

Dear Mum

please don't ever give me porridge for breakfast again. It
tastes like glue. It doesn't taste any better with syrup on
it so please don't try to give it to me again.

I would like Coco Pops instead.

Your loving son (only if you stop making porridge)

Richie

Dear Mum,

Happy Mothers Day. I hope you like your card.
I made it in Mrs Kilburn's class. You are a good
mummy because you buy me nice things and give me
good food to make me grow up big and strong.

I also like riding my bike with you in the park.

Love you lots and lots
Scot xxxxxxxxx

Dear Mummy

I have put some special seeds in the garden with Daddy. He says that when it is your birthday they will all be flowering and smelling really nice for you. It is for a surprise. Daddy told me not to say anything to you. That is why I'm writing a letter instead.

Love you lots and lots and lots
   Alice xxxxxxx

Dear Mum,

Can I not eat sausages anymore please? I have gone off them because Justin Turner says that they're made out of pig toes.

   Lots of love
      Sadie xxxx

Dear Mum

I'm writing this while you're at parents'
evening with Dad. I try to be good but I
know that I'm not always good. When
you come home I will be in my bedroom in
case you got told that I'm naughty. If Mr
Stanley says that I put Robert Howarth's
coat in the toilet it wasn't me it was
Carl Spencer.

Love from Gareth
xxx

Dear Mum,

Was everything in black and white when you were
young like on old films?

Loads of love
Maryanne

Dear Mum,

I am so glad that you're not like Natasha's mum who makes her eat 'moosily bits' for breakfast. She says it's the stuff that bread is made from before they put it together properly when they make real bread. Thank you so much for buying real bread and not making us eat the floury, gritty bits before it's cooked.

All my love
Alicia

xxx

Dear Mum,

Thank you for playing with me and singing songs and for looking after me. I love you very, very much. You are nicer than Kirsty's mum and Helen's mum.

Lots and lots of love
Megan

Dear Mum,

If you try to make me eat green things I will run away. I mean it. I have saved up £12.85 from my pocket money so I can afford to.

Love from Taylor

Dear Mum,

We have finally reached Llandudno after two boring hours on the coach. Sara Pickering was sick when we stopped at the service station. We are going to visit the park and then the castle. I will tell you all about it when I get home.

Lots and lots of love
Julia

Dear Mum,

Please stop telling me to be careful!

Love from Louisa
xx

Dear Mummy,

Please will you always be my mummy and still look after me when I'm grown up because I think I will still need you to.

> **Love and big hugs**
> **Alexandra**

♡⚡

Dear Mum,

I know that you love me and you said that I can tell you anything so I'm going to tell you that Suzy pushed me at school today. I don't know why. I only gave her a little bite on her arm because she wouldn't let me have a turn on the computer. Mrs Jacobs was very cross with me but I don't think that it's my fault.

> Lots of love, Julia
> xxxxxxx

Dear Mum,

I am not cold and don't like to wear so many clothes at once. Please stop telling me that I am going to be cold when I know I'm not.

Love Teresa

Dear Mum

I am writing a letter to you because I want you to write me a letter. Please will you put it in the post box so that the postman brings it?

Lots and loads of loves and kisses
        Beth

        xxxxxxxxxxxxx

Dear Mum,

At school today we did P.E. and Mr Forbes said that we had to climb to the top of the rope but I didn't want to so I hid in the library but then Mrs Jefferies found me and I have a letter to bring home. Here is the letter. I am in my room.

    love
       Rachel

Dear Mum,

I know that you and dad don't have much money so I want to tell you how happy I am with the Christmas presents you have bought me. I have always wanted a kite and an umbrella that you can see through if you put it over your head. I am very happy and I love you lots and lots.

From your daughter Lottie

xxxxxxxxxxxxxxxxxx

Dear Mum,

I really like it on Sundays when we have roast potatoes. Please can we have them everyday?

Love you loads
Carrie

xxxxxx

Dear Mum,

I am sorry that I ate all the ice-cream. Rosa said that she wanted some or she would go home and not play with me so I let her eat it. I don't mind staying in my room whilst it's supper because I'm not hungry.

Love Karen

xxxx

Dear Mum,

I am writing you a letter because I'm at Grandma's house. I like it here but I'd rather be with you. Grandma is really nice and she makes good chocolate cakes. I have been helping to ice them and I have been eating the icing too. It's yummy.

Lots and lots of love
Sophie xxxxxxxxx

Dear Mum,

I just want to tell you how much I love you. Also at school today we did measuring in feet but I can't tell whether they mean big feet like yours and daddy's or small ones like mine.

Love, love, love to you
Olivia

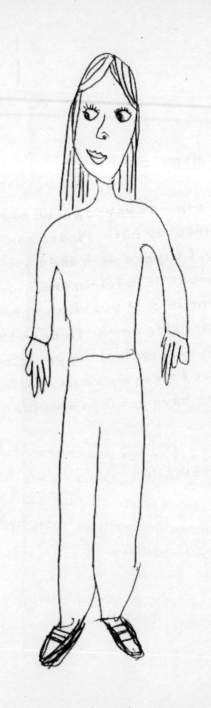

Dear Mum,

I put some of your special bubble bath into my bath. Please don't be angry. I slipped with the bottle and then most of it fell in and there were lots and lots of bubbles everywhere. They are also on the floor in the bathroom. I am leaving you this note because I am in my room and don't want to have got into trouble.

from Lily

Dear Mum,

I have been shopping with Auntie Paula and Frances. Auntie Paula bought me and Frances the same dress but mine is a bigger size because I am older. We saw a man painting the lines on the road. It looks like a cool job. Maybe I will do that when I'm older.

     Lots of love and kisses
       Jenny
         X X X

Dear Mum,

Mrs Marsland told us that bottles of pills have childproof lids so that children can't open them but how does the bottle know that you're a child?

     Love Dean
         X

Dear Mum,

All my clothes say age 6-7 in them because
I am 7. Why do yours say 12? You told
me you were 35.

      Lots of love
        alicia

Dear Mum,

**If I look at things from upside down
they look funny. It also makes the cat
look scary.**

      Love from Toby

Dear Mum,

I miss Grandma too. I am very sad that she died. I think that she looked like the queen only prettier. I am glad that I still have you to give me hugs. Please don't be too sad. I will always be here to give you hugs too.

Lots and lots of loooove
Helena xxxxxxx

Dear Mum,

Why do old people have funny skin that doesn't fit on their face?

Lots of love
Sarah

xxxxxxx

48

Dear Mum,

I am having a good time here with Gran and Granddad. They let me have bye bye cheerios for breakfast. They are yummy.

Lots of love from
Andrew xxxxxxx

Dear Mum,

Why are carrots orange and most other vegetables green or white?

Lots of love
Simon
xxx

Dear Mum,

Grandma took me to a flea market today but I didn't see any fleas. Maybe they are too small.

Love you lots and can't wait to see you
    from
          Jane

⚡

Dear Mum,

Thank you for sitting with me in the thunderstorm. I am always scared the buzz light-year will strike our house like in films.

        Love you very much
            Debbie xxxx

Dear Mum,

I am doing a project on supermarkets at school. When we go in daddy's car he's always calling people idiots. Why are there more idiots when daddy drives than when you drive?

Lots of love
Graham

Dear Mum,

I am writing to you because you have gone out and Jasmine is looking after me. I hope you have a nice time. I like being with Jasmine but she says she's a babysitter. Why do I need a babysitter? I'm nearly eight.

Loves and big hugs
Madeleine x x x

Dear Mum,

I like it when you make pancakes for me when I am sick. Thank you for looking after me so well when I get poorly.

Lots and lots of hugs and kisses from

Mark

Dear Mum,

When I grow up I want to be a mermaid or a queen.

Love Lucy

Dear Mum,

I am having a great time on my school trip. Mrs Dolton made us hammed sandwiches for our packed lunch. Ruth fell in some nettles and is covered with a rash. Mrs Dolron went looking for some dock leaves but we weren't near the sea.

Love and miss you
Karen xxxxx

Dear Mum,

We are learning about the five senses at school. It made me think of tomatoes. I don't like all five senses of tomatoes. I don't like to taste them. I don't like to smell them. I don't like to see them. I don't like to feel them and I don't even like to hear anyone talking about them.

Lots of love from
Jacob

54

Dear Mum,

Here is my postcard from Grandma and Granddads house.
It has a statue of a fisherman on it. That is because
Grandma told me lots of fishermen got killed when
they went out fishing. I don't know why they didn't eat
something else instead of fish. Then they wouldn't be
dead.

Love you and miss you.
Jamie

Dear Mum,

I love you because you are very good at
teaching me things. Now I know how to
make biscuits and fruit cake so I'll never
be hungry.

Loads and loads of love
Florence xxxxx

Dear Mum,

We have been at our school camp for three days now and the rash from the nettles has gone. For breakfast they gave us bread with eggs stuck to it. It was quite nice but I don't like the idea of it. I am sharing my tent with Lauren Townsend and that is good because she is nice. She says that her mum has twenty pairs of shoes all different colours. I think you have more because in my head I've tried to count them and they are all over your bedroom floor. I miss you and can't wait to see you on Friday but I'm also having lots of fun.

HUGE amounts of love and kisses
    Nicci
            xxxxx

Dear Mum,

Please can you buy me a little brother so that I've got someone to play with?

Big love from
Will

Dear Mum,

I am having a nice time at Jerome's house. His mum made hot chocolate with marshmallows but I didn't eat them because you always told me not to go near marshes because they were dangerous.

Love
Davie

Dear Mum,

Please can I have bunk beds so that I can choose whether I sleep up the stairs or down the stairs? I can then put my toys to bed in the spare bed and they can sleep nicely all night.

Lots and lots of love
Nadine
xxx

Dear Mum,

I am writing a letter to tell you how much I love you. You cook me lots of lovely food except for fish pie that I don't like.

Love from
Gareth xxxxx

Dear Mum,

For my birthday I would like a real life puppy. Not a toy one like Barney.

Love and kisses
Sandra

Dear Mum,

Grandma's house is lots of fun and she knows about everything. We watched a television program about sea creatures last night. It said that some fish are dangerous. Jelly fish look like blobs but they can sting. Electric eels can give you an electric shock. They live in caves under the sea where they can plug in their chargers.

Miss you and love you
Hattie

XXXXXXX

Dear Mum,

It is Mother's Day and I want to tell you just how much I love you. You are a very special mummy and you can do amazing things like making bread like they do in the shops. Kate's mum has to buy hers.

Happy Mother's Day and lots of love

Caitlin xx

Dear Mum,

I really like your Sunday dinners but please stop asking me to eat cabbage. It tastes stinky.

Love from Tamsin

Dear Mum,

Happy mother's day. I have made you a
cake with help from daddy.

  Love you lots and lots
  Caroline

p.s. Daddy tidied up the mess because I
told him I was too small. So if there's any
mess in the kitchen its daddy's fault.

Dear Mum,

I asked Grandma where do babies come from but I think she doesn't know either because she told me to ask you.

Lots and lots of kisses
Clare

Dear Mum,

I love you lots and lots because you are kind and happy. Tim's mum is scary, he told me that she has eyes in the back of her head. I've tried to see them but I think they must be hidden under her hair.

Masses of love
Freddie xxx

63

Dear Mum,

I am sorry that I put flour all over the kitchen floor. I just wanted to play at being on the beach. Daddy has helped me clean it up and I am very sorry and promise never to do it again.

Sorry and lots of love
Kirsty

Dear Mum,

I am having a good time with Aunty Rachel and Uncle Pete and Josie. We came here on an aeroplane. It was amazing. It had wings!

Lots of love
Natasha xxxxxxx

Dear Mum,

I love you so much. I think you are very pretty and kind. When I grow up can I have your clothes? Especially the high heeled silver shoes.

Love from Emma
xxxxxx

Dear Mum,

Happy Mother's Day! I think you are the best mum in the world. I think you are also cleverer than Daddy because you work at work and work at home but Daddy just works at work.

Loads and loads of love from
Tilly

Dear Mum,

I am writing to you because you told
me to stop talking. Please could I have
some fish fingers and chips? I would
also like some blackcurrant juice. And
a kitten.

A lot of love from
Joanna
xxxxxxxxx

Dear Mum,

I think that you love me best in the world, better than other people's mums would. That's why you got me when you wanted a baby girl. I love you more than I would love other people's mums as well so it is lucky that you ended up with me.

> Lots of love and kisses
> Daniella
>
> xxxxx

Dear Mum,

When I grow up I want to be just like you. Then I can have a very untidy bedroom like you do and no one will tell me to tidy it.

> Love you very much
> Love from Leah

Dear Mummy,

I am writing a thank you note for my birthday party. I had a really good time. I wish I could have won all the prizes but it's good that my friends got some presents too. Please don't give any of my birthday cake to Aunty Anita when she comes round because she eats a lot and there won't be any left.

Big big love from
Clara xxxxxxxx

Dear Mum,

I think you are the most perfect mum ever. Inside you are the loveliest mum in the world. On the outside you're almost perfect but you could always have some plastic surgery to make you look better.

Lots and lots of love,
Ella xxxxxxxxxxxx

Dear Mum,

Last night I went with Granddad to the fish and chip shop. The man behind the counter went through to the back to get more fish. I tried to look but I couldn't see any sea in the other room but I could smell fish. Where does the fish come from?

Lots and lots of love
Lucy

xxxxxxxx

Dear Mummy

Thank you for everything you have done for me and for teaching me how to be good. This letter is to wish you Happy Mother's Day. I like it when you give me a cuddle. I also like hot roast beef sandwiches

Lots of love to you now and always and always.

Bella xxxx

Dear Mum,

I am having a good time at Helen's house. They have a blow-up boat and her dad took us to the small river and pulled us along with a rope so it was as if we were sailing properly. Their dog Brillo chased us and got very wet. He tried to get into the boat but we had to keep him out of it.

Love you lot and lots and I'm having fun but I also miss you.

Love from Rosie xxx

Dear Mum,

Yesterday when I was playing in the basement room
I borrowed your shoes so that I could do a painting,
without getting my school shoes dirty with paint, so that
you wouldn't shout at me. I did get some paint on them
though so I've washed them and left them in the shed to
dry. If you can't find them, that's where they are. I hope
they are dry now.

> Lots of love
> Carol xxx

Dear Mum,

Happy Birthday. You have kind sparkly green
eyes and a big smile. I love you very much. I
feel safe and happy with you and I hope that
you do with me too.

> Lots and lots of love
> Janey xxx

Dear Mummy,

Grandma and Granddad have brought
us to Blackpool for the day. It is very
cold and there are lots of ships and
seagulls. One seagull tried to get
Granddad's chips and he had to chase
it away. They are very, very big. I am
scared of them. Everything smells of
fish and chips and sweets. The beach
is very big and full of donkeys to ride.
We have been along the pier and I won
a purple dolphin.

Love you lots and lots,
Suzie
xxxxx

Dear Mum,

I only put manure in my sandals because when Mr Ross from up the road was doing his garden he said that it made you grow. That was why he was putting it on his roses. He said that it might make me grow too so I was having a go at standing in it just to see. I didn't grow yet though.

I will wear them even though they smell bad.

I'm sorry.

Love you very much
Jessie xxxxxx

Dear Mum,

You will never know just how much you mean to us all. You are an amazing mum who is very important to me. I love you so much. Happy Mother's Day.

Love from Karl xxxx

Me

buster

Dear Mum,

We are having a lot of fun here at Grandma's. This morning we took the dog to the park and I did roly-poly down the hill and then ended up in the leaves. Grandma says that I will need a very big bath tonight. I still have sticks in my hair.

Yesterday Granddad put on a funny wig to make us laugh. Grandma calls him Betty when he does that and pretends he's someone else.

Love you and miss you,
Calum
xxxx

Dear Mum,

I want to tell you that I really love you very much. I am glad that you clean my clothes and feed me lots of nice food and look after me. I am sorry that I accidentally pulled down the washing line yesterday but I would have fallen off my bicycle if I hadn't been able to grab it. Thank you for not being too angry with me.

Love for ever and ever
　　　Caroline xxxxxxxxx

Dear Mum,

You are very smiley and that makes me feel happy.

　　　Lots of love from
　　　　　　Jon

　　　　　xxx

Dear Mum

You are the best Mum, always kind, caring and thoughtful to everyone. We both love you with all our hearts and we are happy that we have you.

Lots of love and hugs,
Matty and Milo xxxxx

Dear Mummy,

I like it when I can help you when we go to Asda and I can put the shopping into the trolley. Cathy says her mummy lets her help when she is cooking. Please can I help you? I like your jewellery and when you let me play with it I am happy. You have really nice perfume and you are very good to me.

Love you lots and lots,
Charlie
xxxx

Dear Mum,

Thank you so much for my new shoes.
They are the best shoes I've every had
and I bet I can walk all the way into town
and back when I wear them. I've always
wanted some shoes that are red because
they are the nicest.

Love you lots and lots
        Keighley
          xxx

Dear Mum,

I didn't mean to break your sunglasses. I was playing with Suzanna and she made me try them on and then I made her try them on and then they fell off but it wasn't me it was because Lulu came into the bedroom and jumped on my bed and started wagging her tail and then I fell over.

I am very sorry and I promise that I will never do that again.

I love you lots.

Love from Tessa

Dear Mum,

You are the best mum in the world!! You are always happy, caring, loving and do your best to do everything in the world to make us happy. I could not ask for a better mum. I like it when you help out at school and you always help everyone.

Love you
Millions and millions of Kisses

Cassie xxxxxxxx

Dear Mum,

The best place to be on Mother's Day is with you.
Love you lots and lots
Tim

Dear Mum,

Thank you for coming to see me in the school concert. It stopped me from feeling scared because I could see you.

Lots and lots of love.
Maria

xxxxx

Dear Mum,

I am having fun on my school adventure week. You will have a lot of clothes to wash when I come home. I tried canoeing yesterday but didn't like it much. The food is not as nice as yours so I am missing you. We are coming home on the 18th April.

Lots of love
David

Dear Mum,

Do you remember the time I got off the school bus and was upset because someone made fun of me for liking my cuddly rabbit toys? You told me that she was jealous because she didn't have the same toys and that I should ignore her. This week I still played rabbits with my friend Chloe and she started again but this time I ignored her and carried on playing. Then she stopped making fun of me. Thank you mum.

Love you lots and lots
Ella x

Dear Mum,

Here is my drawing that I did with
my new colour pencils. The one with
a lot of hair is you and the one that
looks like Humpty Dumpty is Daddy.
I hope you like it.

      Lots of love from
      Leila

          xxxx

Dear Mum,

Please can we go to China for our holidays? I really like the food we had on Saturday night and I would like to go to the country where all food is like that.

Love from
Joe

Dear Mum,

I am so happy that you are my mum. I am sorry that I dropped the tin of biscuits. They just seemed to fall onto the floor. It isn't because they were too heavy to pick up like you said. I can carry things heavier than that. I can carry the cat.

Lots of love from
Danny

Dear Mum,

Auntie Carol is looking after me very well. Last night she made mash and sausages for tea. It was very good. I am writing you this letter because Darryl has been sent to her room. Her mum (Auntie Carol) caught her stealing from the special biscuit tin. I was **NOT** doing it so I am downstairs still. It is getting a bit boring.

Loads and loads of love
Jenny

Dear Mum,

This is a proper thank you note
because Mrs Wilkinson says that we
should always say thank you to people
who are good to us so I'm going to
write you thank you for buying me my
new dress and thank you for buying
me my favourite chocolate biscuits. I
would also like a new umbrella.

Lots of love
Lola

Dear Mum,

We are having a great time in Ramsgate. At night in the hostel after the teachers go to bed, we get up and play around in the dark. It is pancake day on Tuesday and we're going to have them for tea. Jimmy banged his head yesterday but Mr Todd says it's not serious and won't affect how stupid he is. I will see you on Friday.

       Lots of love
           Sam

Dear Mum,

We live in the North West.

Love

Harriet

Dear Mum,

**I love you. You're my best friend.
Thank you so much for helping me and
loving me all the time.**

Love from Andrew

Dear Mum,

Cool pens!

Love
      Sasha
xxxxxx

Dear Mum,

I promise that when I am a teenager I will not wear funny black clothes or stay in my room all the time. I will not play bad music very loudly or stay out too late and I will **NEVER, EVER** like boys.

Love, love, love from

Chloe

Dear Mummy,

My favourite cakes are the donuts with pink icing and coloured sprinkles.

Huge love from Katie

Dear Mum,

I think you are great. You are nice to me and you take me places. I like it that you tuck me into bed at night and turn off my light.

Thank you for my kitten, he's the worlds best cat ever.

    I love you lots and lots
    Rachel
    xxxxxxx

Dear Mum,

I really miss you when you go to work.

    Lots of love
    Jamie
    X X X

Dear Mum,

I am me because you are you. Thank you for being you because I like me.

Lots and lots of love
Roberta

Dear Mum,

I like it when we bake buns and I like going to Grandma's with you but I don't like shopping.

Love from Harry

Dear Mum,

I am sorry that sometimes I am naughty. I did not mean to spill paint on the carpet. I tripped over my shoes by the sofa when I was carrying the paints. I am very glad to have you and grateful for how you look after me. I will try to be more careful in future.

Love you lots
Penny XxXxX

Dear Mum,

We are practising writing letters in school so I have to write to you. I am not in a good mood today because Gary Tetlow tripped me up when I went over to the art table. He said it was an accident but I don't believe him because he laughed.

Love from Charlie

Dear Mum,

I know Mr Eastwood has told you that I was bad today and hit Brett McLaren but I want to write to say it wasn't like that. Brett took my key ring with the skeleton on it out of my bag and threw it to Taylor. Taylor dropped it and when I tried to pick it up Brett pushed me over with his foot. That's why I hit him. Mr Eastwood wouldn't listen so now I hate him as much as I hate Brett McLaren.

I love you though.
Love from Daniel

Dear Mum,

We have been on our trip for two days now and I have to tell you that the food is yucky. It is worse than school dinners, worse than cauliflower and worse than dog food. If I have to stay here I will behave like a dog when I get home because of all the bad food I am being given.

Please rescue me from certain dog-life and misery.

Love from Jack

xxxxx

PS Other than the food it is fun here!

Dear Mum,

I am excited to be sleeping over at Caroline's house. We have been to the hospital to see her sister Linda and her new baby. The baby is small and pink and has squashed brown hair. She is called Lily and she didn't open her eyes. Caroline's mum says that it's because the lights n the hospital are too bright because she has just come out of the dark of Linda's tummy. Why do they not make sunglasses for babies who think the light is too bright?

See you on Sunday night. Love you loads and loads and lots of big hugs.

Laura

Dear Mum,

I am so grateful that you look after me and Joe. We would like to give you a present so we have tidied up all the things in the kitchen cupboards. I am telling you that Joe ate the jelly cubes himself and I didn't eat any so I am good. Joe wouldn't give me any.

Lots of love from
Gill xxx

Dear Mummy,

You are my favourite mummy ever. I'm sorry for calling you names and not behaving myself. I am very bored in my room which is why I'm pushing this letter outside for you to read. I would really like to come out and get some flapjacks. I love you very much mummy.

Love, and more love.
Lisa Xxxxxxxxxx

Dear Mum,

I am very lucky for having a mum like you. Thank you for looking after me every day. Grandma showed me some photos of you before you had me. Did you get bored of having nothing to do?

Is that why you wanted me?

Thank you, thank you and lots of love

Julie X

Dear Mum,

I am having a nice time staying at Ian's house. Yesterday, his Mum made us drinks and gave us them with those curly straws. I had to have a pink one, which belonged to Ian's sister. He laughed at me. His Mum made him swap then, so that I had his blue one. I am looking forward to seeing you again.

Loads of love from Andy

Dear Mummy,

You have always looked after me really well. I like being with you and miss you when you have to go somewhere without me. I still remember you dropping me off at nursery each morning and me feeling sad when you had to go. Now I am bigger and at school and I know that you are coming home to me and that you haven't left me behind. I hope you will always look after me.

Lots of love and kisses
Tessa x x

Dear Mum,

Today dad took me to a football match. It was a draw but it was fun to watch. Afterwards we went to a café and had fish and chips. It is getting cold so dad bought me a scarf. We are coming home on the train on Thursday. I have bought Sam a toy bus that is also a pencil sharpener and I have bought some soap for you that smells nice.
It is a present.

Lots of love
Dan

Dear Mum,

Thank you for coming to the school
swimming competition. Are you proud
that I won? I am.

Love from Bradley
xxx

Dear Mum,

Thank you for being brighter than the sun.

Lots of love
Tallulah
xxxxxxxxxxxxxxxxxxxxxxx
xxxxxxxxxxxxxxxxxxxxxx

Dear Mum,

I am so sorry that I was being bad yesterday and I will try not to be such a baby in future. I just don't like it when you spend all your time looking after my little sister and tell me to look after myself. I like it best when you look after me.

Love from
Stevie XXX

Dear Mum,

You are the best mum ever. I like to go to the park with you and I like it that you are good at climbing trees with me. Whenever I need you you always come to me. You are very kind.

Lots and lots of love
Erin xxxx

Dear Mum

I am sorry for being mean to you when I wanted to play football in the garden and you said it was too wet. I don't really want to get muddy. I think that mostly you are very kind to me.

Love from
Paul xxxxx

Dear Mum,

Thank you for helping to tidy the school library. It is much easier to find things now.

Love from
Sammy

Dear Mum,

Janine's birthday party was fun. Her dad said he is a sock broker and you can tell because he didn't have any shoes on and his socks have a lot of holes in them. It didn't look nice. I'm not going to be a sock broker when I grow up.

       Lots of love
          Lizzie

Dear Mum,

I love you and I will always. I like it when you give me one of your big hugs. Nobody can hug me like you. I am going to do my best at school like you said. Thank you for everything you do for me.

    I love you with all my heart.

      Love from Stella xxxx

Dear Mum,

Please can I have a rabbit? Sara at school has a rabbit and it can play with her in her room. It is brown with big floppy ears and I love it and would like one for my birthday. I don't think the dog will be too upset.

Love Tara

xxxxx